WOMEN
IN
HISTORY

PEACE & WAR
1900-1945

FIONA MACDONALD

Chrysalis Children's Books

This edition published in 2003 by
Chrysalis Children's Books
The Chrysalis Building, Bramley Rd, London W10 6SP

ISBN 1 84138 887 4

British Library Cataloguing in Publication Data
for this book is available from the British Library.

Series editor: Claire Edwards
Editor: Angela Royston
Series designer: Jamie Asher
Designer: Zoe Quayle
Cover Designer: Keren-Orr Greenfeld
Picture researcher: Diana Morris
Consultant: Ann Dingsdale

Printed in Hong Kong
10 9 8 7 6 5 4 3 2 1

Picture Acknowledgements
AKG London: 19t, 22l, 26t, 26b, 33c, 37b, 40bl, 40cr, 43b.
British Library/Bridgeman Art Library: 9b.
Coo-ee Historical PL: 11t, 44t.
Corbis-Bettmann: back cover l, 6c, 7t, 18br, 20t, 21t, 21b, 25br, 29b, 31cl, 33b, 34t, 34b, 35b, 38c, 39bl, 41t, 42b, 44b, 45c.
Mary Evans P.L: 10b.
Fawcett Library/Mary Evans P.L: 11b.
Fox/Hulton Getty: front cover cr, 3l, 25t,.31br, 32b, 36cl, 36b.
Hulton Getty: front cover b, 3c, 3r, 5tr, 6b, 9t, 10t, 12b, 13t, 13b, 14c, 14b, 15b, 17c, 17b, 18cl, 19b, 20b, 23t, 23b, 27br, 29t, 42c, 43t.
John Jesse, London/Bridgeman Art Library: front cover cl, 3cr, 25tbl.
Keystone/Hulton Getty: 16c, 28b, 41b.
Roy Miles/Bridgeman Art Library: 16b.
National Army Trust, Pennsylvannia/Bridgeman Art Library: 37t.
North Wind: 3cl, 4b, 5cl.
Private Collection/Bridgeman Art Library: back cover tr, 3cl, 8b, 15t, 30r.
Tony Sarno/Corbis-Bettmann: 38b.
Reg Speller/Hulton Getty: 39br.
Topical Press/Hulton Getty: 1c, 8c, 24b.
TophamPicturepoint/Bridgeman Art Library: 12c.
Tretyakov Gallery, Moscow/Bridgeman Art Gallery: 27tl.

CONTENTS

Setting the Scene   4

War and Revolution   12

Women and Politics   18

Post-war World   24

Return to Old Values   28

The Great Depression   32

The Second World War   36

Women of Achievement   42

Glossary and Further Reading   46

Index   48

Peace and war

Europe and America changed rapidly during the first half of the twentieth century. It was a time of war and peace, progress and disaster. Governments were strong, trade and industry were growing fast, motor cars and aeroplanes and other exciting scientific discoveries were being developed. But there were also revolutions, strikes and protests, sudden economic crises, and two terrible world wars. As opportunities arose, masses of women seized them, changing their lives as never before.

> *I myself have never been able to find out precisely what feminism is. I only know that people call me a feminist when I express sentiments that differentiate me from a doormat [opinions that show I am not a doormat].*
>
> REBECCA WEST, ANGLO-IRISH WRITER, 1913

A golden age?

Looking back, people often call the years 1900 to 1914 a golden age. Compared with the horrific world war that followed, in which over 10 million men died, life before 1914 was peaceful and pleasant for many in Europe and the USA. Britain, France and Germany each ruled a worldwide empire. The USA boldly and bravely claimed that it was the 'land of opportunity' and the 'home of the free'.

Not for everyone

But life was not easy for everyone in this golden age. Everywhere, there was a wide gap between rich people and poor people – in income, living standards, comfort, health and even life span. In the USA, there was still racial discrimination in many states, even though slavery had been abolished in 1865. And there was no country on Earth where women were equal with men.

This woman is operating a complicated loom to weave patterned cloth. Even though she is skilled, she earns less than her male colleague. In 1900, women's wages were always lower than men's.

How wealthy women lived

In rich households, most women did not go out to work. But they still had a job to do. They were expected to make a good impression and to further their husband's career, by dressing well and socializing with people 'who mattered'. Just a few well-educated women worked as doctors, nurses, senior teachers and journalists.

By 1900, almost half the teachers in American primary schools were women. This class is at a school for black pupils in New York.

Ordinary women

Among ordinary families, many young, unmarried women worked as domestic servants, cooking, cleaning, and caring for sick people and children. Other working-class women laboured in factories, or in sweatshops (dark, crowded workrooms), or did piecework at home. Countrywomen laboured on farms. Better-educated women became shop assistants, office clerks, telephone operators and junior teachers. Married working-class women did two or more jobs – they were home-makers, cared for their husbands and children, and went out to work for wages as well.

American heiress Jennie Jerome married a British nobleman. Their son was Winston Churchill, later Britain's famous wartime leader. Wealthy young women were expected to 'catch' good husbands and make careers as wives and hostesses.

1900–1914	Golden age of peace and economic growth. Peak years for migration to the USA from Europe and Russia.
1914–1918	First World War
1917	Communist Revolution in Russia
1920s	Peace and rapid social change. Age of Flappers (liberated young women).
1930s	The Great Depression – a serious economic crisis affecting the USA, Europe, and many other lands. Rise of warlike fascist political movements in Europe.
1939–1945	Second World War.

What did women want?

Throughout the nineteenth century, strong-minded women in Europe and the USA had campaigned for equality with men. They had achieved much, but in 1900, women were still not treated equally in many important areas of their lives. Women campaigners particularly wanted better pay, better conditions at work, and the right to vote.

Women are one-half of the world, but until a century ago ... women lived a twilight life, a half life apart ... it was a man's world. The laws were men's laws, the government a man's government, the country a man's country. Now women have won the right to higher education and economic independence. The right to become citizens of the state is the next and inevitable consequence ... We have gone so far; we must go farther. We cannot go back.

M CAREY THOMAS, AMERICAN WOMEN'S COLLEGE PRINCIPAL, 1908

Dangers at work

In 1900, more women worked outside their own homes than ever before. Many women welcomed the independence from husbands and fathers this gave them, but factories and sweatshops were often dangerous places. Fingers and hair were trapped in fast-moving machinery. The air was filled with choking steam, cotton dust or dangerous chemical fumes. In Britain, the government passed laws to protect women workers from the worst of these dangers, but many women still damaged their health, or lost their lives, in factories.

Women workers in a hat-making factory in England, 1909. They are crowded uncomfortably close together. The air is damp, stale and full of fabric fibres, which irritate their lungs.

Social reformer Emma Goldman speaking to a crowd in New York in 1916. She is campaigning for women's equality and workers' rights.

Unions and strikes

In 1900, American women campaigners founded the Ladies' Garment Workers Union, to demand better pay, as well as safer conditions. They organized many strikes and protests. Women members of the National Consumers' League organized boycotts, refusing to buy goods from factories where women workers were badly treated. Even so, tragic accidents like the Triangle Shirtwaist Disaster showed the shocking conditions in which many women still worked.

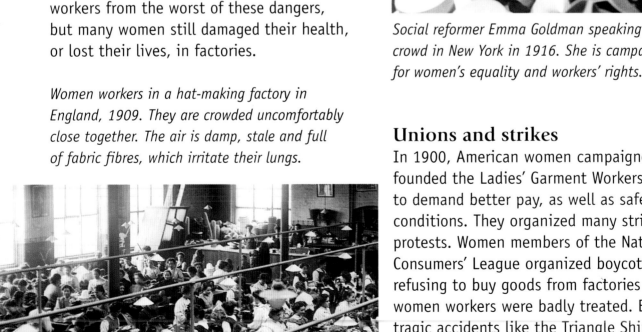

The Triangle Shirtwaist factory after the fire (see right). The factory had been designed to house as many workers and machines as possible, with no thought for health or safety.

THE TRIANGLE SHIRTWAIST DISASTER

On 25 March 1911, a fire broke out in a New York sweatshop where 500 young women worked. The fire quickly spread, as cotton waste and sewing-machine oil burst into flames. The sweatshop's owner had locked all the doors, for fear the workers would steal the shirts, and the women were trapped inside. Panic-stricken, the women jumped out of windows; 146 were killed, and many more were badly injured.

Civil rights

In 1900 women had no political power, except in New Zealand and a few US states. Voting would allow them to choose who governed them, and to have a say in how their taxes were spent. They also wanted to serve in public office and as jurors in law-courts. In 1900, women government ministers seemed an impossible dream.

1900: Legal Rights

• In Britain and many states of the USA, married women had won the right to keep their own property and wages. (Before, these had belonged to their husbands.) They could also inherit a share of their husband's property when he died.
• Women were acknowledged by law to be joint guardians of their children. (Before, they had no legal right to see or care for them.)

BUT:
• In the USA, the 14th Amendment to the Constitution guaranteed equal rights only to all males, not to all citizens.

1900: Education and Careers

• Most girls went to school, and could read and write, but most left at 12 or 14 years old.
• Women had won the right to train as teachers, nurses, doctors and college lecturers.

BUT:
• Women were banned from many careers, such as law, architecture, the army, police force, and the church.
• Women were often paid only half as much as men and were not given top jobs.
• Many employers forced women to stop working when they married.

Votes for women

'Sensible and responsible women do not want to vote,' declared former US president Grover Cleveland in 1905. He was wrong. Women had been demanding the vote since 1850. By the 1900s, many thousands of women were joining suffragist groups, such as the British NUWSS (National Union of Women's Suffrage Societies) and the NAWSA (National American Women Suffrage Association). They demanded equal voting rights with men.

Suffragists carrying flags in a Wake Up America parade in 1919. They marched through New York, demanding the right to vote.

Peaceful persuasion

In America, suffragists – often led by young college-educated girls – went from door to door, explaining their views. They toured cities in trams and buses, making speeches. Crowds gathered to stare at their scandalous behaviour (as respectable people saw it). These American campaigners vowed that the topic of votes for women would be in the newspapers all the time. They held a wide range of opinions. For example, some black women's groups wanted to link winning the vote with wider civil rights campaigns.

Time to act

Until 1900, most women in Britain also hoped to win the vote by patient, peaceful persuasion. They were led by Millicent Fawcett, who wanted to show that women could win without using threats or violence – the typical weapons of men. A few British campaigners did not agree. They wanted to take direct action. In 1903, Emmeline Pankhurst, with her husband and daughters, founded the WSPU (Women's Social and Political Union). Its main aim was to make people and the government take notice of them until they won the vote for women. The Pankhursts attracted many followers, who became known as suffragettes.

What a Woman may be, and yet not have the Vote
MAYOR · NURSE · MOTHER · DOCTOR or TEACHER · FACTORY HAND

What a Man may have been, & yet not lose the Vote
CONVICT · LUNATIC · Proprietor of white Slaves · Unfit for Service · DRUNKARD

A British suffragette publicity leaflet, 1911. It asked why responsible, hard-working women were not allowed to vote, while irresponsible, sometimes dangerous, men could vote.

Emmeline Pankhurst making a passionate speech. Although some people disapproved of the Pankhursts' wild words and militant actions, they won great publicity.

Good or bad?

Even today, people disagree about whether suffragette tactics worked. Many people in 1913 thought they had gone too far. The British government said it would never give in to their demands, for fear that other groups, such as militant trade unionists and Irish Republicans, would start similar violent campaigns. Many women left the WSPU and joined the non-violent NUWSS instead.

Militants

The suffragettes used many tactics to gain publicity. In 1905, they interrupted political meetings, especially when government ministers were speaking. After 1906, they deliberately tried to be arrested and sent to prison. They were careful never to use violence against people, but from 1908, they decided to attack property – mostly by smashing shop windows or damaging men's sports grounds.

Violent protests

In 1913 suffragettes carried out many violent protests. They set fire to post-boxes and railway buildings, cut telegraph wires, and poured purple dye into public drinking-water reservoirs. A suffragette hurled an axe at the Prime Minister, only just missing him. The nation was shocked when campaigner Emily Davison threw herself under the King's horse at an important race-meeting. She died from her injuries a few days later.

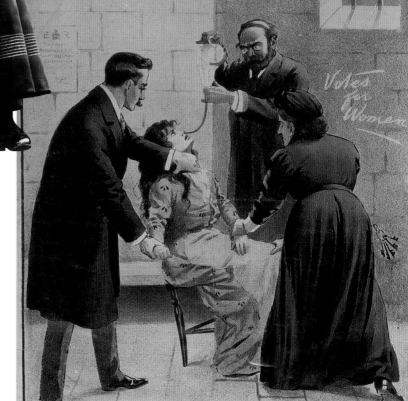

Many suffragettes were sent to prison. There they continued to protest by going on hunger strike. This poster speaks out against the force-feeding of women prisoners.

Around the world

By 1918, women in Western Europe and America had made their demands very clear. Around the world, many other women were also campaigning for change. Sometimes, their aims were similar to those of women in the West. Sometimes, they had different ambitions. But everywhere, they proved that women were full of vision, responsible, and worthy to be trusted with power.

South-east Asia

Women in south-east Asia focused their campaigns on two main targets: equal educational rights for women, and freedom for their country to govern itself. (At this time, many nations in south-east Asia were ruled by Europeans, as colonies.) In India, for example, Sarojini Naidu (1879–1949) worked closely with Mahatma Gandhi, campaigning for independence from Britain. She organizing peaceful protests while Gandhi was in prison. In the Philippine islands, Melchora Aquino began her political activities when she was 83, by sheltering rebel soldiers. The islands became independent of Spain in 1898.

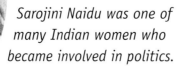

Sarojini Naidu was one of many Indian women who became involved in politics.

Chinese women with bound feet in the early 1900s. Teacher Ch'iu Chin (1879–1907) opposed this traditional but painful custom, and worked to improve education for Chinese girls.

China and Japan

In the Far East, two very different kinds of revolution were taking place in the early twentieth century. In China, rival groups of nationalists and communists struggled for power. Among the nationalists, sisters Soong Ching-Ling and Soong Mei-Ling worked as secretaries and close advisers to the two main nationalist leaders. Among the communists, student Chen Tiejin led the revolutionary Red Guards, was captured, and executed aged only 24. In Japan, there was a social revolution as men and women challenged traditions that had shaped their lives for hundreds of years.

Australia and New Zealand

European women who settled in Australia and New Zealand worked very hard in their new homeland. Living in wild, harsh countryside, they had to be tough and resourceful to survive. They felt they had earned the right to be treated equally with men. Rose Scott (1847–1925) led demands for women's votes in Australia. She did not marry, saying 'life is too short to waste on the admiration of one man'.

Vida Goldstein (see right) campaigned for women's rights at work and in the family.

Africa

In many parts of Africa, women were not equal with men, but they had important traditional powers. In Nigeria, for example, women traditionally managed the trade in markets and ports. European administrators wanted to remove their powers. But Nigerian women, led by 'Market Queen' Omu Okwei and teacher Fumilayo Ransome–Kuti, refused to co-operate. As a result, women still control much of the trade in West Africa.

Fumilayo Ransome-Kuti opposed European attempts to limit the right of African women to run the markets and ports in Nigeria.

SOME CAMPAIGNERS FOR CHANGE

India
Pandita Rambai (1858–1920) campaigned for women's right to education and to train as doctors.

Philippines
Josepha Abiertas (1894–1929) was a lawyer who campaigned for equal rights for women in the new Filipino state.

Japan
Motoko Hani (1873–1957) described women's real lives in newspaper articles. This broke an ancient taboo and was deeply shocking.

Australia
Vida Goldstein (1869–1949) campaigned for property rights in marriage and for divorce reform.

New Zealand
Kate Sheppard (1848–1934) pioneered outdoor sports, and campaigned for votes for women.
Harriet Morison (1862–1925) organized trades unions for women.

Aboriginal women

Aboriginal women, belonging to the earliest peoples who inhabited Australia and New Zealand, faced different challenges. How could they prevent their ancient beliefs and ways of life from being destroyed by the Europeans, and keep hold of their traditional farms and hunting grounds? Women like New Zealand Maori campaigner Princess Te Puea set up welfare schemes for women and children, and encouraged Maori people to preserve their traditional customs and skills.

First World War

Events in Serbia in 1914 drew Germany into war against Russia and France. The First World War led to the worst fighting ever seen in Europe. It involved Britain, Australia and many other nations. Most campaigners stopped demanding votes for women and joined in the war effort. They wanted to support their men and show how responsible women could be.

Let us show ourselves worthy of citizenship, whether our claim to it be recognized or not.

MILLICENT FAWCETT, 1914

I am an enemy of war because I am a feminist. War represents the triumph of brute strength, while feminism can only triumph through moral strength and intellectual values ...

PEACE CAMPAIGNER HELENE BRION, 1918

Nursing care

Everyone – men and women – believed that nursing was women's work. In Europe, existing hospitals were reorganized, ready to admit men injured in war, and many large public buildings and private houses were turned into temporary hospitals or nursing homes. Thousands of young women volunteered to help.

A nurse chats to soldiers who have been blinded in the war. Women nursed injured men back to health, and cheered them up as well.

Advertisers have always used pretty girls to help sell their ideas. The message on this US recruiting poster was clear – 'real men' should join the navy.

GEE !!
I WISH I WERE
A MAN

I'd JOIN
The NAVY

BE A MAN AND DO IT
UNITED STATES NAVY
RECRUITING STATION

In the war zone

The First World War was unlike any other war. Enemy armies spent years living in muddy trenches and fighting over land known as the Front Line. Women were not allowed to go to the Front Line, but many worked behind the line in army hospitals as nurses and ambulance drivers. They worked in difficult conditions, caring for casualties brought in from the battlefield.

A mother says goodbye to her soldier son. After the US joined the war, one American woman wrote, 'It is easier to die than to send a son to death.'

Home comforts

Women also provided simple comforts for soldiers. They ran canteens for troops home on leave, and packed boxes with warm woollen socks, chocolate, a few cigarettes, and friendly messages. These were collected by the army and delivered to troops on the battlefield. Officers' wives even managed to send food parcels of delicacies to their husbands from famous luxury shops.

Emotional support

Women's emotional support was also vitally important to men who were away at the war. Many soldiers carried a signed photograph of their girlfriend, sister or mother in their uniform pocket, or a loving letter from home. Cheering and encouraging troops as they marched off to war was often very difficult for women. They knew that their sons, brothers or boyfriends might well be killed.

Women against war

A few women campaigned against war. They believed that wars, which were almost always started by men, should be banned. They wanted quarrels to be solved by peaceful, calm discussion. Leading women peace campaigners included French schoolteacher Helène Brion and Jeannette Rankin, the first woman elected (in 1917) to the US Congress.

EDITH CAVELL

Edith Cavell (1865–1915) was born in England and trained as a nurse. in 1907 she went to Belgium to be head of a nursing college. When German armies invaded Belgium during the First World War, Cavell turned the college into a Red Cross hospital. Like all Red Cross workers, she and her staff cared for injured soldiers, whatever their nationality. She was arrested by the Germans, and shot as a spy because she let British and French troops shelter in her hospital. Her dying words became famous. She said 'Patriotism is not enough…'

Nurse Edith Cavell was honoured for her bravery and for her care of all injured men.

Women replace men

Traditionally, wars were men's work. Women did not fight battles. But during the First World War, from 1914 to 1918, women proved that they could do other vital jobs just as well as men.

Carry on, carry on, for the men and boys are gone,
But the furrow shan't lie fallow while the women carry on ...
[furrow means ploughed field; fallow means left without crops]

JANET BEGBIE, WARTIME SONG 'CARRY ON'

Women take over

In most European countries, young men were conscripted (made by law to join the armed forces). So many were sent to fight, there were not enough men left at home to do their usual peacetime jobs. Women took over, running shops and offices, delivering mail, driving trams and buses, and working on farms. They took on heavy work, labouring in coal mines, shipyards, and brick-factories. Some quickly learned the skills needed to become carpenters, tool-makers and engineers.

In wartime, women proved that they could be trusted with skilled, responsible jobs. This woman is driving a tram in France in 1917.

New kinds of work

The war also created new kinds of jobs – assembling guns, packing ammunition, filling shells with explosives, and building aircraft. This work was urgent and vitally important. Women were often asked to work 12-hour days in government factories, and they were carefully watched and timed. Men's lives might be lost if women worked too slowly, or made mistakes.

Dangerous work

Much war work was unpleasant and very dangerous. The chemicals used to make explosives were poisonous – they burned the skin and irritated the lungs. Hundreds of women died through working with them. Paints and varnishes used to make aircraft and lorries also gave off harmful fumes, which made women workers very sick.

A British Ladies Fire Brigade puts out a blaze in 1916. Before the war, most men had assumed that women were scared of heights, and too weak to handle heavy ladders.

A poster calling for women volunteers to work on farms. Women's organizations such as the YWCA (Young Women's Christian Association) were very good at organizing war work.

Proving their worth

At first, many men thought that women would be too frail to do a full day's work, or too thoughtless and silly to act responsibly. Men who had not yet gone to war protested, and even threatened to go on strike, when women workers were sent to join them. But women proved these critics wrong. They kept the country running almost normally, while the men were away at war.

FLYING WOMEN

The First World War was the first war in which aircraft played an important part. Pilots (all men) flew over enemy land to spy on soldiers and tanks. But a few daring women were also interested in flying. So in 1917 Helen Gwynne-Vaughan organized the Women's Army Auxiliary Air Force. Specially-trained women went to France, where they maintained and repaired the British Army's few, precious warplanes.

American women's war work

Women in America also joined in the war effort, even though the USA did not fight until 1917. The largest votes-for-women organization sponsored a soldiers' hospital in France. Leading campaigners knitted army socks in public. Well-known women, such as silent-film star Mary Pickford, asked people to buy Liberty Bonds to help pay for the war. One million ordinary American women worked in war-factories.

Before the war, women received no technical training at school. But in wartime they quickly learned new skills.

The Russian Revolution

In 1905, Russian workers, soldiers and peasants started a revolution against the Tsar [emperor], but it failed. It was followed by protests and strikes. In 1917, there were two more revolutions. The first, led by moderate liberals, removed the Tsar from power. The second was led by Bolsheviks (communists who were ready to use violence to win power). Women played an important part in these revolutions and suffered as much as the men.

> We, the women of Russia, who are living at this great time of Russia's renewal ... appeal to male honour and conscience, and demand ... civil and political rights equal to men's.
>
> RUSSIAN WOMEN'S UNION DEMAND, C. 1905

Women protesters, armed with guns, marching through the streets of St Petersburg, Russia, during one of the revolutions in 1917.

Communists seize power

In 1917, in bitter winter weather, Russian women queuing for bread staged more protests against the government. They were joined by communist factory workers and by soldiers and sailors, angry with the way the government was handling the war. Together they attacked government offices and the Tsar's old palace. The communist leaders were impressed by the protesters' strength and decided that the time had come to seize power.

Rights and reforms

When women protesters demonstrated in front of the Tsar's Palace in 1905, they were fired on with machine-guns by the palace guards. For most of these women, demands for political reform were linked to demands for women's rights. Revolutionaries such as Alexandra Kollontai spoke to women working in factories. They told officials that they were going to talk about women's health and child care. In fact they spoke about workers' freedom and women's rights. The factory-workers eagerly supported them.

Before the revolutions, women from wealthy Russian families lived very comfortable lives. This painting, by Russian artist Ilya Efimovich Repin, shows his wife, children and a woman servant in a large, well-furnished room.

Changes!

The revolutions in Russia changed women's lives dramatically. After the first revolution in 1917, Russian women were given equal rights with men, including the right to vote. After the second revolution, Bolshevik leaders created a special *Zhenodtel* (women's office) within the government. As Minister of Welfare, Alexandra Kollontai introduced new laws giving women equal rights within marriage, and the chance of a fair divorce.

After the communist revolution in 1917, women were appointed to many official jobs in the new government. Here, a female election supervisor helps a woman to cast her vote.

ALEXANDRA KOLLONTAI

Alexandra Kollontai (1872–1952) became convinced that the Russian political system under the Tsar was wrong. She wrote protest stories, joined a workers' movement, left her husband and young son, and went to Switzerland to study economics. She became a Bolshevik, and campaigned for women's rights.

After the Tsar was overthrown in 1917, Kollontai returned to Russia, and was made Minister for Welfare. She was the only woman minister in the revolutionary government and the first female government minister in the world. The Bolsheviks admired her spirit and some of her ideas, but not her independent mind. In 1923, they sent her away from Russia as an ambassador and she spent the rest of her life abroad.

Women and men working side by side at a telephone exchange during the revolution of 1917.

Revolutionary ideas

There was a price to pay for these benefits. After 1917, all women (including mothers) were expected by law to work just as hard as men, all their lives, in state-run factories and farms. Many women felt this was a fair deal. But they did not agree with Kollontai's idea to end marriage and families altogether and to let the state bring up children and care for old people instead.

17

The vote – at last

After the First World War, women in Britain and America finally won the right to vote equally with men. In the USA, the 19th Amendment to the Constitution (1920) declared that no citizen should be banned from voting 'on account of sex'. In Britain, a law passed in 1918 allowed women over the age of 30 to vote. Ten years later, all women over 21 were allowed to vote.

> Women … have proved themselves able to undertake work that before the War was regarded as solely the province of men … Where is the man now who would deny to women the civil rights which she has earned by her hard work?
>
> BRITISH MALE GOVERNMENT MINISTER, 1916

American suffragists in 1917 picketing the White House, home of the President of the USA. They demanded the right to vote.

How the vote was won

In the USA, votes-for-women protesters had stood outside the White House for six months in 1917. In the end, President Wilson himself agreed to ask Senators and Congressmen to accept their demands. The British government was impressed with women's war work, but nervous about headstrong young women. At first they agreed to give only older women the vote.

Why now?

There was no single reason why men (who controlled politics and law-making) decided to give women the vote. Women's long, patient years of campaigning in local and national associations played an important part. So did the violent demonstrations of the suffragettes – though they discouraged many men, too. But the most important reason of all was the way in which women in Britain and the USA had behaved during the First World War.

Carrie Chapman Catt (1859–1947) organized the American campaign to win the vote.

18

Minds of their own

Men could no longer claim that women were too fragile or too stupid to be trusted with the vote. No one could believe that a woman's place was in the home, when women had been seen digging coal, driving lorries and making bombs. Although many men had disliked working alongside women at the beginning of the war, some had learned to respect them as equals.

Hopes for the future

To women everywhere, voting meant that they were publicly recognized as equal citizens, and could play a full part in politics. Women also hoped that voting would open the door to new opportunities – in work, education, and public service. They hoped it would encourage governments and employers to treat them as men's equals in other ways too.

Women campaigned for the vote in many European countries. This Dutch cartoon shows women confronting their prime minister in 1918.

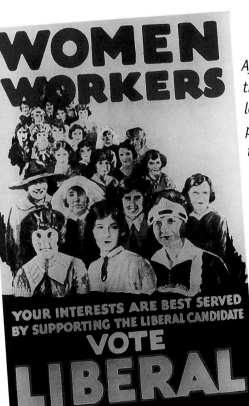

After women won the vote, male-led political parties asked for their support. This poster shows new, young British women voters in 1931.

WOMEN'S VOTING RIGHTS WORLDWIDE

Britain and America were not the first nations to give women rights to vote:

1893 New Zealand (the first ever)
1902 Australia
1906 Finland
1915 Denmark
1917 Russia
1918 Britain (for women aged over 30)
1919 Netherlands
1920 USA, Czechoslovakia
1921 Sweden
1928 Britain (for women aged over 21)
1931 Spain
1932 Brazil, Uruguay, Thailand, the Maldives
1933 Turkey
1934 Cuba
1941 Panama
1944 France

Women helping women

Even after women won the vote, they continued to join local and national groups to help other, less fortunate, women, or to achieve their shared aims.

Welfare work

During the 1890s, wealthy American and British women had helped found Settlement Houses in poor, run-down city areas. Settlements were designed as community centres. They offered help on welfare issues, and classes on subjects from basic hygiene to office skills – and sometimes music and art. They often had canteens where cheap, nourishing food was served.

Mother and baby clinics

Women doctors, nurses and unpaid helpers also worked together in mother and baby clinics. They gave free advice on child health and nutrition to women who could not afford to see a doctor. Some clinics were criticized because they also offered contraceptive advice to married women.

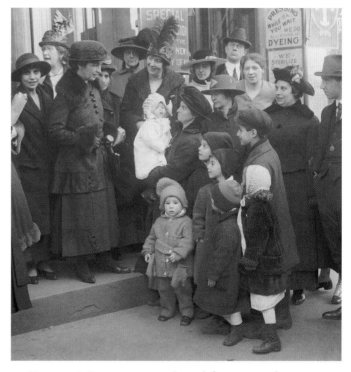

Margaret Sanger campaigned for women's health and set up special clinics for mothers.

Self-improvement

Many clubs and societies provided help, education and company for women and girls. In Britain, the Mothers' Union combined prayer and Bible reading with discussions on children's education and family welfare. Other groups such as the Women's Institute had no religious connections, but encouraged women to broaden their outlook by hearing talks on travel, fashion, current affairs and the arts.

Guides and Scouts

Clubs for teenage girls, especially the Girl Guides and Girl Scouts, became popular in the 1920s and 1930s. The ideal guide or scout was fit, active, educated and capable, dressed in a short skirt and with windblown hair. This was a huge change from the ideal girl of 1900, sheltered and dressed in a long, heavy frock, with her hair pinned neatly into place.

British Girl Guides preparing a meal while camping on the beach at Le Touquet in France in the 1920s.

American campaigner Alice Paul (1885–1977) played a leading part in winning votes for women. She led the National Women's Party, and suggested an Equal Rights Amendment to the US Constitution in 1916.

MARY MCLEOD BETHUNE

Bethune's parents had both been slaves. Bethune (1875–1955) worked on cotton plantations until she won a scholarship that allowed her to go to college. She worked as a schoolteacher, then married, and decided to set up a school of her own for poor black girls. The school did well and in 1923 merged with a nearby school for black boys, to become the Bethune-Cookman College. Bethune also helped set up small businesses and a housing improvement scheme. In 1936, she became the first black women to hold a major government office.

Equal rights

Winning the vote was an achievement for women, but it was not the end of their struggle. In America, women's organizations, especially the National Women's Party, began a campaign for the US Constitution to be amended to give women equality in all areas of life. Today their aim has still not been achieved.

Black women's rights

For many members of the US National Women's Party, equal rights did not always mean black people's rights. Black and other ethnic minority women often campaigned for their own rights alone. Determined women such as Mary McLeod Bethune worked hard to improve education and jobs for black young people, especially girls.

Mary McLeod Bethune (on the left of the picture) at a meeting with Eleanor Roosevelt, wife of the US President. Both women helped disadvantaged people and became close friends.

Women with power

Women campaigning for the right to vote also demanded the right to be elected to national governments – to Congress and the Senate in the USA, and to the House of Commons in Britain. They wanted to be involved in making policy as well as voting on it.

First steps

Until 1900, hardly any women had political power. The only exceptions were rulers, such as Queen Victoria of Britain who died in 1901. Women married to powerful men, such as presidents and state governors, sometimes managed to influence their husband's opinions, and even to make them change their minds. But they had no legal right to do this, and were often hated for it.

First mayoress

Very rarely, a woman whose husband had died was allowed to carry on his local government work, and in this way women proved that they could handle power. For example, in 1907, pioneer doctor Elizabeth Garrett Anderson took over as mayor of a small English town when her husband died. She was so successful that the town council invited her to stand as a candidate in new elections in 1908. She won, and became mayor in her own right.

Winning national elections

The first woman elected to national political power in America was Jeannette Rankin, who became a Republican member of Congress in 1917. She was a supporter of votes for women, and was well known for her hard-working campaigns. She travelled vast distances on horseback to meet the voters. She was a trained social worker and tried to introduce laws to protect women and children. She lost her seat after opposing America's entry into the First World War.

Helene Weber was a member of the Prussian (North German) government until 1933, when the Nazis forced her to resign. In 1946 she returned to politics and won great respect.

Lady Astor was the first British woman to take her seat in Parliament. Here she speaks to women students in 1925. They played an important part in politics after women won the vote.

Members of Parliament

The first British woman MP to play an active part in Parliament was an American, Nancy Astor. She was married to a wealthy Englishman, and was elected in 1919, as MP for the port of Plymouth. She served as an MP for more than 20 years. She supported laws that would help women and children, and campaigned against alcohol abuse because of the harm it did to many families.

Still a minority

Rankin, Markiewicz (see box) and Astor were all outstanding women. Generally, voters in Britain and the USA were cautious about voting many women into power. Local political parties seldom chose women as candidates. At the 1931 general election in Britain, there were only 67 women candidates competing for about 400 seats as MPs. Of these, just 15 were elected.

THE REBEL COUNTESS

The first British woman MP was Countess Constance Markiewicz (1868–1927). She married a Polish nobleman, and was a passionate and active supporter of independence for Ireland. She was condemned to death for carrying a gun and commanding a troop of soldiers, but this sentence was changed to life imprisonment. In the 1918 general election (the first when British women could vote) Markiewicz was elected to Parliament as an MP for Dublin, even though she was still in prison. She was re-elected several times but, as a protest against Britain's rule in Ireland, refused to attend the British Parliament.

Countess Markiewicz campaigning for votes in Dublin in 1922. She is surrounded by children, probably members of the 'Na Fianna', the Irish independence youth movement she founded.

Bright young things

Few people, men or women, lived through the First World War without suffering. When the war ended, they felt scarred and saddened yet also very relieved. Peace in 1918 brought a new sense of hope, and dreams of new possibilities. How did these affect women's everyday lives?

> No time to marry, no time to settle down I'm a young woman, and I ain't done running around…
>
> FROM 'YOUNG WOMAN BLUES', SUNG BY BESSIE SMITH, 1927

Freedom from rules

For women who had lost their husbands peace often brought money worries and loneliness (see page 27). Young single women also mourned their dead brothers and friends, but, as survivors, they wanted to make the best of any new opportunities. They broke the old rules of respectable behaviour. They wore daring new fashions, and went out alone or with men, without a chaperone (older woman) to watch them.

Leaving home

Sometimes, if they could afford it, young single women even left their family home to live alone, or with other female friends. This was a big change. Before the war, almost all unmarried women lived with their families or in their employers' homes.

Flappers

These liberated young women were known as flappers or 'bright young things'. To them, the old rules for good behaviour seemed ridiculous. The rules were meant to protect young ladies from the harsh realities of life. But women who had spent the war doing difficult, dangerous work, or nursing soldiers in army camps no longer needed protection. Winning the vote made women even more scornful. What right had men – or society – to limit what they could do?

A crowd of bright young things riding in a stylish new car. A women driver was rare in the 1920s.

Entertainer Josephine Baker was bold, defiant and sometimes shocking, but she expressed what many young people felt.

WOMEN AND SPORT

In the 1920s many women seized the chance to play tennis, hockey and golf, to run, dive and swim, drive sports cars and fly dangerous planes. Before the war, men had said that women lacked strength and the urge to compete. They also said it was not decent for women to show their arms and legs or look sweaty in public.

By the 1920s, sportswomen no longer cared what men thought of them. They wore short, loose frocks or trousers (this was very shocking), so they could move easily. Pioneer sportswomen, such as Suzanne Lenglen (from France) and long-distance pilot Amelia Earhart (from the USA), became world famous and were admired by men and women.

Having fun

As wage-earners, young women could spend their own money on clothes, music and exciting entertainment. There was new music, such as wild, rebellious jazz and soulful blues, and there were dance crazes, such as the energetic Charleston. There were nightclubs, fashions and new, fast cars.

Suzanne Lenglen is still respected as one of the world's greatest tennis players. She played with elegance and style as well as athletic skill.

An illustration from a fashion magazine, showing styles of the 1920s. Women no longer forced themselves into tight corsets, but wore clothes that were comfortable and easy to move in.

New jobs for women?

As the First World War ended in 1918, 3000 British women working in wartime jobs were asked what they wanted to do with their lives. Almost all of them said they would prefer to stay on in their new jobs, rather than return to old-fashioned women's work. This was not the answer the British government wished to hear. It urged women to give up their wartime jobs, so that there would be work for returning soldiers.

Back to the old ways

By the end of 1919, there were hardly any women still doing war work. Women with husbands, or who came from wealthy families, gave up full-time work altogether. Single women returned, very reluctantly, to prewar jobs such as cooking, cleaning, caring for children or working in shops and offices. There, they earned much less than they had in wartime, and were treated with less respect.

A woman schoolteacher and her pupils in Germany in 1921. Women teachers were respected, but not usually highly paid.

New careers

Women teachers, nurses and doctors were now fully accepted by almost everyone. Increasing numbers of women found work in other professions – as librarians, college lecturers, and academic researchers. A few exceptional women did manage to make new careers for themselves. Some of the earliest studies in women's history were written at this time by women historians. Women explorers, such as Jacquetta Hawkes and Margaret Mead, journeyed to remote places to study lost civilizations and peoples with very different lifestyles from their own.

A secretary at her desk in 1921. She is young and probably single. Women were expected to stop work when they married.

Women artists pioneered dramatic new styles. This bright, challenging oil painting was created by Russian woman artist Liubov Popova. It was called Spatial Force Construction 1921.

Artistic talent

Women writers worked as journalists, novelists and in the new – very popular – film industry. Women with artistic talents, such as Sonia Delaunay and Eileen Gray, set up studios where they made and sold paintings, pottery, fabric and furniture in startling new designs. Women designers such Coco Chanel and Elsa Schiaparelli also won many admirers. Schiaparelli's clothes were witty and dramatic, and she also invented the colour shocking pink. Other women set up small shops selling feminine goods such as hats, clothes, shoes or babywear.

WOMEN WITHOUT MEN

More than 10 million men were killed in Europe during the First World War, and more than 20 million were seriously injured. This meant that a whole group of men aged between 15 and 40 years old had died. They left millions of grieving widows and girlfriends.

Some widows did not want to remarry. They preferred to cherish their husband's memory and look after their children. But they had little chance of finding another partner anyway. Most single women in the 1920s knew that they would have to spend their lives without men, which also meant without children. At that time, it was unthinkable for a respectable woman to have a child outside marriage.

Life was not easy for women whose husbands had been killed in the war. They often had to bring up their family on very little money.

RETURN TO OLD VALUES

Women and trades unions

Since the early nineteenth century, women had joined trades unions. But in the 1920s and 1930s trades unions were still dominated by men. Many working men were suspicious of women who wanted fulltime, lifelong careers.

Jobs for men

Most men in the 1920s and 1930s did not think that equal pay and jobs for women were nearly as important as finding jobs for men – especially soldiers. Governments and trades unions saw women's demands for equality as a threat. If women were given jobs, then more men would be out of work.

> A trade unionist – of course I am. First, last, and all the time. How else to strike at the roots of the evils undermining the moral and physical health of women?
>
> MAUD YOUNGER, A WOMAN TRADES UNIONIST

The family wage

Most men also believed in the idea of a family wage. They thought that the proper way to organize an economy was to pay one person in each family – almost always the man – enough to feed, clothe and house all the people who depended on him. If a woman worked then her money was for extras. She should either spend it on things to help the family (a new cooker, maybe) or save it for a rainy day.

Women taking part in a Hunger March in 1932. Trades unionists from many parts of Britain marched to London, demanding the chance to work or welfare to feed their families.

These women in Vienna, Austria, joined together in the 1920s to form a co-operative (a company they ran themselves) for maids and servants.

Few women belong

These attitudes meant that few women in the 1920s and 1930s belonged to trades unions. Even fewer were trade union officials, with the chance to shape union policy and change men's minds. (There were one or two exceptions to this rule – for example, in the garment industry in the USA.) But women within the trade union movement, such as Red Ellen Wilkinson, did all they could to improve wages and conditions for women workers.

Wider issues

Trades unions also linked women's demands at work with wider issues of equality. They were active in women's education. For example, American union leader Ella Barker organized the Workers Educational Program which ran summer schools for women factory-workers at top women's colleges.

Members of the Garment Workers' Union picketing a shop in San Francisco, California. They were campaigning for better conditions and pay.

RED ELLEN WILKINSON

Wilkinson (1891–1947) was nicknamed Red Ellen because of the colour of her hair and because red is the colour of revolution. She was the daughter of a British cotton-factory worker, who won a scholarship to university, campaigned for votes for women, and became a public speaker for the Independent Labour Party. In 1915, she became organizer for the Amalgamated Union of Co-operative Employees. She worked hard to help low-paid workers, especially women.

Wilkinson briefly joined the Communist Party, then became a Member of Parliament – the first woman Labour Party MP. All her life she campaigned for justice and social change. She was Minister of Pensions and Minister of Education, but she continued to support the trades unions and the unemployed.

29

Good wives and mothers

By the 1930s, many 'bright young things' (see page 24) were changing, maturing and slowing down a little, and new ideas about women became fashionable. People began to suggest, once again, that a woman's place was in the home.

Unfair!

There were many reasons behind these new ideas. Some were economic. After 1930, many industries faced serious problems, and millions of men were unemployed (see page 32). It seemed most unfair to them that some women were still working.

The woman who can move about a house,
Whether it be a mansion or a camp,
And deftly lay a fire, and spread a cloth,
And light a lamp
And by the magic of a quick touch give
A look of home to wherever she may be
Such a woman will always seem
Great and beautiful to me.

GRACE NOLL CROWELL

Right-wing ideas

New ideas about women were also connected to new political theories, particularly right-wing ones. (People with left-wing political views were more likely to see women as equal to men.) The most extreme right-wing theories, known as fascism, were popular in Germany, Italy and Austria. There men were encouraged to be warriors. One German leader summed up women's role as 'Church, Children, Cooking'. These ideas were never popular in the United States, but they had some influence there.

A popular British magazine from 1933. For women who did not go out to work, home-making and child care were topics of great interest, in which they could show skill and creativity.

Mothers of the race

In European countries with overseas empires, some politicians argued that it was women's duty to stay at home as wives and mothers of the race. Although this sounds shocking today, they believed that Europeans had a God-given right to rule other parts of the world. To do this, a steady supply of young men were needed. By raising boys to serve the empire (and girls who would marry them) mothers were performing an important task.

Upper class

Staying at home was also a matter of class. If a woman stayed at home, it was a sign of wealth and refinement. It showed that her husband earned enough, or owned enough, to support his whole family. Some men insisted that their wives stay at home, even though they were really quite poor. Sometimes their wives were pleased to have the chance to show off their status. Others found it a burden.

A middle-class American family in about 1940. The husband and children are seated and eating. The wife is serving their food.

Glamour and charm

The idea of woman as homemaker also appealed to many women. By the 1930s, there was a new generation of young women, born shortly before the First World War. Unlike their mothers or older sisters, they had not worked in challenging wartime jobs, or campaigned for the vote. They wanted to be glamorous and charming, not tough and strong. And they now had the chance to marry and raise children of their own.

Swedish filmstar Greta Garbo was a leading example of 1930s glamour and charm. She was cold and mysterious, but many men thought that her womanly beauty was attractive.

THE GREAT DEPRESSION

The crash – and after

The 1920s were a time of hope and new ideas. New businesses were set up, and seemed to be booming. But in 1929, the US stock market suddenly crashed. Share prices fell, making many people's savings worthless overnight. Families and companies were ruined, and the American economic crisis (often known as the Great Depression) spread to many countries round the world. What impact did this have on women?

> *While you're living in your mansion, you don't know what hard times mean; Poor working man's wife is starving; your wife is living like a queen.*
>
> FROM 'POOR MAN'S BLUES', SUNG BY BESSIE SMITH, 1930

Out of work

The most damaging effect of the stock market crash was that millions of people lost their jobs. Businesses in many countries collapsed. People lucky enough to keep their jobs found that their wages fell. Employers could not afford to pay them well – but they also knew that workers were afraid to ask for more money, in case they were sacked.

Dole queues

In the cities, men and women queued for hours at employment offices, hoping to be offered work of any kind. They also queued for cheap meals, cooked and served by charities. They begged in the streets, or tramped from business to business, desperate to find a job. Many families became homeless and lived on the streets, or sheltered in railway stations or other public buildings. The fortunate ones found beds in welfare centres.

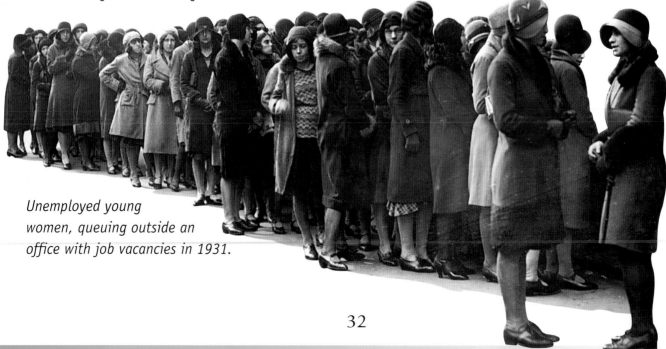

Unemployed young women, queuing outside an office with job vacancies in 1931.

Women come last

Many people had no money to pay for food, so farmers around the world lost their incomes too. Farmers could not afford animal feed, or seeds and fertilizers to grow crops. On farms and in cities, women traditionally put their families first. In the Depression, this meant going without food, shoes or warm clothing, so that their children would be warm and fed. Husbands, trades unions, governments and employers all put pressure on working women to give up their jobs, so that men could work instead.

Tensions

Money worries often led to tensions between husbands and wives. Men felt worthless if they could not provide food and a home for their families. Faced with ruin, men committed suicide, became violent towards their wives and children, asked for a divorce, or simply left home. Life for unemployed couples was miserable. For deserted women and their children, it could be even worse.

WOMAN WITH VISION

Dorothea Lange (1895–1965) was a photographer who showed the rest of the world how US farm-women and their families were suffering during the Great Depression. Her photos showed the women's determination and strength, as well as their suffering. Lange's photos were part of a project sponsored by the government to record the lives of farming families. They helped to win support for Roosevelt's New Deal welfare programme to help the poor (see page 34).

Dorothea Lange took this photo in 1938. It shows a poor American mother fanning away flies from her baby's face with a cap.

A farming family in America shelters in a tent. During the terrible years of the Depression, many farmers lost their homes and their land.

Slow recovery

During the 1930s Depression, women did their best to cope with unemployment and poverty. If their families still had money, they gave food or volunteered to help with welfare schemes. Even women who had almost nothing assisted one another in the best way they could. But governments in many countries realized that charity and voluntary work was not enough. Poor people needed help from the state to survive, and governments had to help to rebuild the economy.

Women in Memphis, Tennessee. During the 1930s, many US women were forced to stay at home. By law, only one family member could have a job.

The New Deal

In the USA, where the Depression had begun, President Roosevelt and his wife, Eleanor launched a welfare programme known as the New Deal. It helped the poorest groups in society: poor women and black people. He also appointed Frances Perkins, as Secretary of Labor.

Frances Perkins (1882–1965) was the first woman government minister in the US. She introduced new laws covering social security benefits, wages and working hours.

Not for women

Some countries of Europe also passed welfare laws, but few were as wide-ranging as the New Deal and many benefits did not apply to women. For example, in Britain there were groups who could not claim unemployment pay. These included most married women and many workers in women's jobs, such as domestic servants or cleaners. Women who lost their jobs and refused to do domestic work were paid no welfare benefits.

A long way from victory

Many women during the 1930s felt they were further away than ever from achieving equal rights with men. They had the vote, and laws governing marriage, divorce and children were less unfair. But women's wages were still much lower than men's and hardly any women were promoted to senior jobs.

Women, unite!

Women also felt discouraged for another reason. Ever since the vote was won, there had been no single issue on which they could all agree. Now, in the 1930s, there were many women's organizations, all with their own views and plans. They disagreed about religion and politics. Campaigners feared that unless these groups could unite women would never win equal rights.

ELEANOR ROOSEVELT

Roosevelt (1884–1962) was born into a wealthy, powerful family, and devoted her life to helping women, children, black people and the poor. At 17, she took on unpaid work with children. Aged 21, she married a distant cousin, called Franklin Roosevelt, who had political ambitions. When Franklin became ill, and had to use a wheelchair, she helped him to continue his political career (he was elected President in 1932). She acted as his assistant and advisor. She also continued with her own social work career, writing and speaking on welfare issues. In 1933, she toured the USA to tell people about her husband's New Deal policy.

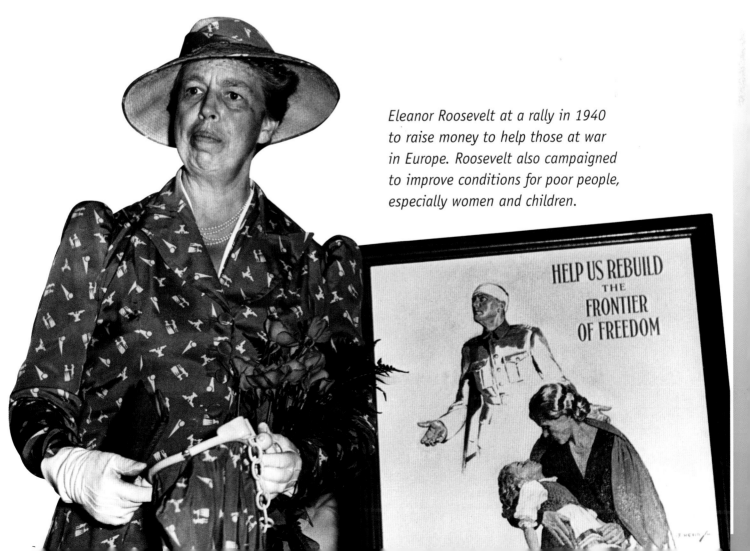

Eleanor Roosevelt at a rally in 1940 to raise money to help those at war in Europe. Roosevelt also campaigned to improve conditions for poor people, especially women and children.

HELP US REBUILD
THE
FRONTIER
OF FREEDOM

Women at war

In 1939, Britain and many other European nations were once again at war with Germany. Germany's main allies were Italy and Japan. America joined the war on the British side in 1941. This conflict became known as the Second World War. Women did not fight, but worked closely alongside men to help them plan and prepare for battle.

Never Underestimate the Power of a Woman
COVER SLOGAN, LADIES HOME JOURNAL, 1941

Women in the Canadian Army change the wheel of an army car in 1943.

Women join forces

For the first time, governments in Europe and the USA organized large numbers of women into special branches of the armed forces. In Britain in 1939, for example, there were 3400 women in the Women's Royal Naval Service, 8000 in the Women's Auxiliary Air Force, and 24 000 in the women's branch of the British Army. Many more young women joined later in the war.

Life in uniform

Women in the forces wore uniforms and lived in barracks and camps, just like men. They were trained to march and obey orders, though not to fire a gun. At first, many women were given typically female tasks to perform, such as cooking, cleaning, nursing and secretarial work. But later, women were trained as drivers, mechanics, motorbike couriers, photographers, and radar operators. Women serving with the Air Force were trained in map-reading and navigation, so they could track enemy aircraft as they flew across the sky.

A woman motorbike rider carries urgent instructions or information to officers at army headquarters.

This image of a patriotic, reliable woman was used to recruit women to the US Army.

Help from America

In 1941, after America joined the war, the American government also enrolled women to support their fighting troops. Although American women did not fight in the front line, they were often sent to the war zone shortly after the men. In 1944, Technical Sergeant Mabel Carney won praise as the first American service woman to arrive at the battlefields of Normandy after US troops invaded German-occupied France.

Women pilots

Women also used their expert skills to help the war effort. American pilot Jacqueline Cochran flew a bomber across the Atlantic (an exhausting and dangerous task) and volunteered for service with the British forces. She became an officer in the British Air Transport Auxiliary. This special group flew warplanes from the factories to the air bases. It included many women.

These women pilots, wearing helmets, goggles and thick coats, are ready to fly aircraft for the Russian Air Force in 1943.

Rosie the Riveter – and friends

Rosie the Riveter was a character in an American wartime song, written to encourage women to join the war effort. But most women did not need much encouragement to volunteer. In the USA, nearly half of all women, including mothers of young children, worked during the war. In the UK, nine out of ten single women and eight out of ten married women took part in war work. Once again women proved that they could, like men, carry out heavy, dirty, dangerous tasks.

Making war machines
In Europe and the USA, war was becoming increasingly technological, and Britain and its allies needed an enormous number of war machines. Women were sent to aircraft factories, engineering works, chemical and weapons factories. There, they cast, cleaned, cut, polished and carefully fitted together the thousands of parts that made up war machinery – from guns and gas masks to planes and tanks.

She's the girl that makes the thing
that drills the hole that holds the spring
That drives the rod that turns the knob
that works the thingumebob.
... And it's the girl that makes the thing
that holds the oil that oils the ring
That works the thingumebob
THAT'S GOING TO WIN THE WAR!

POPULAR SONG, UK, 1942

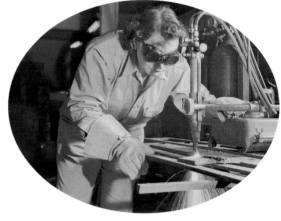

A woman worker using new skills and precision cutting equipment in a British arms factory.

Riveters and welders
As the song (above) shows, everyone relied on women to work quickly and accurately. In shipyards, women worked as welders, riveters and crane drivers. In bomb factories, they handled dangerous chemicals and assembled delicate electrical equipment such as fuses and timers.

In 1944 this US railway worker's boss said, 'The gals are as good as the men ever were.'

Replacing men

As in the First World War, women also did everyday jobs left by men who had gone to war. They drove buses, trains and heavy lorries. They repaired bomb-damaged buildings, worked in factories and small businesses. They worked long hours, sometimes all day and all night, taking short catnaps in rest-rooms or canteens. Many women with young children also worked.

Working for the government

Some women worked for the government as administrators, typists and translators. They prepared government advertisements and radio broadcasts. In Britain, a few highly intelligent women were chosen to become part of a team gathering information about the enemy. They listened to enemy radio signals, and helped to break the enemy's secret codes.

LAND GIRLS

In Europe and America, there was a shortage of food during the war. The situation was especially bad in Britain, because it usually relied on food imported from overseas. Now enemy battleships patrolled the coasts, so as much food as possible had to be grown at home. In Britain, female farm workers were known as Land Girls. They worked long hours and often ended up sleeping in haylofts or converted cattle sheds. But working out of doors, in noisy, lively all-girl gangs, could be an exciting experience. In the first year of the war 25 000 land girls signed on.

As well as growing food and caring for animals, Land Girls also learned to drive tractors, handle chemical pesticides and fertilizers and service farm machines.

US mathematician Grace Hopper works on an early computer. Women's skill with codes and numbers helped to win the war.

The Home Front

Women, and all those who stayed at home, were also part of the war. The British government called them the Home Front. Life in Europe was very difficult indeed. Bombing destroyed cities, and millions of people fled from the Nazis and became refugees. Millions of Jewish people who could not leave German-occupied lands were killed in death camps.

Death and destruction

In the Second World War, civilians (men, women and children not in the armed forces) suffered almost as much as fighting men. Planes from both sides bombed cities, reducing them to rubble.

Whatever happened, women had to feed their families. These women look for shops selling food in badly bombed Berlin, Germany, 1944.

Living with bombs

Women and children saw their homes destroyed and their neighbours killed. Often they remained homeless for years. Faced with the nightly threat of bombs, women did their best to protect their families. In big cities, many families left their homes and went to sleep in huge public shelters.

Children were evacuated from London in 1939 to avoid being bombed. Many would not see their families again for several years.

Evacuees

Some parents decided to send their children away from home, for safety. Thousands of Jewish children were sent from mainland Europe to Britain and America, to escape persecution. They often never saw their parents again. In Britain, the government evacuated children from cities into the countryside. Women in quiet country areas took city children into their homes.

Soldiers drew glamorous images of women on warships, tanks and planes. The pictures reminded them of wives and girlfriends back home.

Make do and mend

Feeding and clothing a family was difficult. Many foods – such as meat, fish, sugar, eggs and butter – were rationed and fresh fruit was hard to find. Fuel, clothes and cleaning materials were also rationed. Women were encouraged to make do and mend, for example, by making slippers out of old felt hats, or unravelling spare woollen sweaters to knit warm blankets or children's clothes.

The end of the war

By the time the Second World War ended in 1945, many women's lives had changed for ever. They had lived through hardship, shortage and stress. They had done hard, dangerous work and learned new skills. They had lost loved ones. Now they faced an uncertain future. What would the postwar world be like?

History repeats itself

To older women, who had been alive in 1918, history seemed to be repeating itself in 1945. As men came back home from fighting overseas, women were asked to give up their wartime work. Married women were encouraged to stay at home. Unmarried women were expected to take less responsible, low-paid jobs. In spite of women's wartime efforts, their legal situation had hardly changed at all. Women were still not equal with men.

WARTIME FASHION

Wartime clothes for women were short and simple, to use as little fabric as possible. Often they looked like men's uniforms, creating the impression that women were in the forces, too. Popular hairstyles were given fighting names, such as the victory roll. Make-up and stockings (tights were not yet worn) were in very short supply, so women improvised, staining their lips with berries, and using crayons for eye make-up. They drew a seam in black crayon up the back of their legs to look as if they were wearing stockings. For the first time, it became acceptable for women to wear trousers in public. They were warm and practical.

British wartime fashions in 1942. Sensible, heavy shoes, short skirts, and jackets looked like army uniforms.

WOMEN OF ACHIEVEMENT

Women in media and the arts

For many centuries, women had painted, sung, written poems, letters and diaries, and sewed beautiful clothes. But it was only after 1900 that a career in the media or the arts became acceptable for a woman. Here are just a few of the many women who won praise and fame – and sometimes made their fortunes – from these new careers.

Ida Wells Barnett (1862–1931)

Born a slave, and orphaned at the age of 14 years, Barnett became one of America's most outspoken journalists. At first she worked as a teacher, but lost her job when she complained about the way black people – including herself – were treated. She went to work on newspapers in Memphis, New York and Chicago, and led campaigns against lynching (the murder of black men by gangs of white people who accused them unjustly of crimes). In 1909, she was one of the founders of the National Association for the Advancement of Colored People. This became a leading civil rights organization in the United States.

Marian Anderson

Lady Rhondda (Margaret Haig Thomas, 1883–1958)

Daughter of a wealthy businessman, Haig Thomas was a keen supporter of the suffragettes in the UK. She took part in demonstrations, was imprisoned and force-fed. After her father died, she took over his business and ran it successfully. She also fought for and won the right to inherit his title and sit in the House of Lords. In 1920, she founded the feminist weekly magazine *Time and Tide*, inviting many famous thinkers and politicians to write for it.

Marian Anderson (1897–1993)

Born into a poor family in Philadelphia, Anderson started singing in church when she was six years old. In 1925, she won first prize in an international singing competition. This led to a concert tour of Europe, and worldwide fame. But, because she was black, Anderson was barred from singing in one of America's most famous venues, Constitution Hall in Washington. Her outraged fans arranged an alternative concert for her instead, which was a great success.

42

Gabrielle 'Coco' Chanel (1883–1971)

Chanel (right) came from a poor farming family in France. Her parents died when she was very young, so she lived with an older sister. They survived by working for a hat-maker. Chanel learned fast, and opened a hat-shop of her own in 1912. After the First World War, she moved to Paris, and began to make clothes for rich women. Her designs soon became popular. They were based on casual, simple shapes and used stretchy knitted fabrics, that were flattering and easy to wear. By the late 1930s, she was the wealthiest fashion designer in France.

Kathe Kollwitz (1867–1945)

The daughter of a left-wing preacher and the wife of a doctor, German artist Kollwitz used her powerful art to help people in distress. Her black-and-white prints and sculptures were designed to show the miserable lives led by many poor people. She was opposed to war, and many of her finest works are about wartime grief and death. She designed a war memorial to her son, who was killed in the First World War. In 1928 she was elected Professor at the Prussian (North German) Academy in 1928. When the Nazis came to power in 1933, Kollwitz was forced to resign, but she still went on working at home. She was killed during a bombing raid during the Second World War.

Mary Pickford (1893–1979)

Born in Toronto, Canada, Pickford worked as a child actor, on the stage. She made her first film aged 16, and soon became Hollywood's most popular female star. Because she was young and pretty, people called her the nation's sweetheart, but she was also an intelligent business woman. In 1916, Pickford set up her own film company, because she preferred to be independent of the big studios' control. 1n 1919, she and three others formed United Artists, which became one of the most powerful film-making companies in the world. Pickford won an academy award as Best Actress in 1929, and retired a few years later. In 1975 she was given a special award to honour her unique contributions to the film industry.

Anne Frank (1930–1945)

Frank was born in Germany to a Jewish family. When the Nazis gained power the Franks left Germany to live in Amsterdam in the Netherlands. Anne lived an ordinary life until the Nazis invaded the Netherlands in 1941. The Frank family went into hiding in tiny rooms behind their warehouse. Neighbours risked their lives to bring them food secretly. Frank kept a private diary of her life, thoughts and feelings at that time, which she hid in her room. In 1944, the family were betrayed to the Nazis and taken away to concentration camps, where Anne, aged 15, died of disease. After the war ended, Anne Frank's diary was discovered and published. It is still read today as a tragic reminder of the horror of war.

Women pioneers

After 1900, pioneering women worked to change the world in many ways. Some made important new discoveries; some campaigned for health and welfare; some followed exciting new careers.

Alexandra David-Neel (1869–1968)

David-Neel spent her early years in Paris, where she became fascinated by East Asian objects in museums. In 1888, she inherited money, and used this to visit India and North Africa. At that time, very few European women travelled there alone. In 1911, her husband gave her more money for travelling, and she studied languages and religions in India and Tibet. She journeyed in dangerous, remote mountain regions, unknown to Europeans. She spent a whole winter in a mountain cave with Buddhist nuns, and three years in a monastery in Beijing. In 1923, in disguise, she became the first European woman to enter the forbidden city of Lhasa, in Tibet. She wrote many books about her travels, and finally returned to Europe in 1936.

Daisy Bates (1861–1951)

Born in London, Bates worked with the Aboriginal people of Australia to fight for their rights. Europeans did not understand Aboriginal culture and lifestyle, and wished to destroy them. Bates spent 35 years living as a nomad, alongside Aboriginal families. In 1935, she wrote about the fast-disappearing Aboriginal way of life, so that it would not be forgotten. She went on campaigning until she was 85.

Annie Jump Cannon (1863–1941)

Cannon was born in Delaware, and received a good education at two leading women's colleges. In 1896 she took a job as an astronomer at Harvard Observatory, where she worked for the rest of her life. Her task was to help compile a photographic catalogue of all the known stars. Cannon developed a system for examining star photographs, which became used by most other astronomers worldwide. She was appointed senior astronomer at the Observatory in 1938. She was one of the few women elected to the American Philosophical Society.

Annie Jump Cannon (right) with Caroline E Furness

Irene Joliot-Curie (1897–1956)

Daughter of Marie Curie, one of the world's most famous scientists, Joliot-Curie was an outstanding researcher in radioactivity and a professor at one of the top French universities. In 1935, she won the Nobel Prize, the world's highest scientific award. Joliot-Curie also spent time away from the laboratory. She was opposed to fascism, and became a member of the anti-fascist French government in 1936. She supported many feminist causes, and argued that women should have the right to join the French Academy of Sciences – the association of leading scientific scholars. Joliot-Curie used her expert knowledge to help the French government develop nuclear power. But she was opposed to nuclear weapons and campaigned for world peace.

Bessie Coleman

Bessie Coleman (1893–1926)

Coleman was born of poor parents in Atlanta, Texas. She was the first woman to qualify for an international pilots' licence. But, because she was black, American flying schools would not accept her and she had to go to Europe to take the pilots' exams. During the First World War she worked in France for the Red Cross. When the war was over, French Army pilots taught her to fly. She returned to the USA in 1922 to earn her living by giving demonstrations in flying. She died in a flying accident when she was only 33 years old.

Maria Montessori (1870–1952)

Montessori was the first Italian woman to qualify as a doctor, in 1894. She then worked with children with learning difficulties, and saw how they learnt by exploring the world around them. From 1907, Montessori used her observations to develop a new way of teaching, based on children's natural curiosity. She encouraged learning through play. It was a revolutionary change from the usual teaching methods of that time. Many people thought Montessori's way of teaching would not work, but it was a great success with all children. She travelled round the world, telling people about her ideas. She set up colleges to train teachers. Today, there are Montessori schools and colleges in many lands.

Amelia Earhart (1898–1937)

Born to a lawyer's family in Kansas, Earhart planned to be doctor. But, after she was offered a trial flight at an air show, she decided to change careers and become a pilot. She felt sure that flying would give women independence and new ways of earning money. In 1928 Earhart achieved worldwide fame by becoming the first woman to cross the Atlantic by plane, as navigator to a male pilot. Earhart soon set many other records, including the first non-stop flight from Hawaii to California. In 1932 she flew solo across the Atlantic. In 1937, Earhart was flying the last quarter of a record-breaking flight around the world, when her plane disappeared over the Pacific. It has never been found.

GLOSSARY

Aboriginals The original inhabitants of a country.

barracks A building where soldiers live.

bereavement Feelings of sadness because someone has died.

Bolsheviks Members of a Russian political party who demanded revolution. After the second revolution in Russia in 1917, they formed the first Communist government.

boycott To refuse to have anything to do with somebody or something, as a protest against a policy or injustice.

campaign An organized group of activities, such as speeches or marches, designed to change peoples' views or to win new rights.

career A job with opportunities for progress, training, more responsibility and more pay.

civil rights The rights that allow an ordinary person to play a full part in society, such as the rights to vote, to receive an education, to have a job and to follow their own religious faith.

communists People who believe in a system of government in which there is no private property. Instead, the government owns and runs everything on behalf of the people.

concentration camp Place where thousands of people, especially Jews, were imprisoned in terrible conditions by the Nazis.

congressmen Member of the national law-making assembly of the USA. It is made up of two chambers, the Senate and the House of Representatives. Both have to agree on all new laws.

conscripted Made by law to join the armed forces.

conservative Wanting to preserve the way things are and opposed to changing them.

constitution The ideas and principles by which a country is governed. Some countries, such as the USA, have a written constitution.

demonstration A public protest.

economic Having to do with the management of money.

equality Having the same rights and opportunities as others in a group or society, and being treated with respect and as an equal.

evacuated Moved out of a dangerous area to a place which is thought to be safer.

evacuees People who have been evacuated, especially in a war.

family planning Deciding how many children to have, and when to have them, usually by using contraception or other forms of birth control.

fascism A political theory based on beliefs in a strong leader and on the right of the state to control all aspects of individual women's and men's lives.

left wing Having radical, socialist views.

liberals People who hold tolerant views on a wide range of issues.

Liberty Bond A bond issued by the US government to raise money to fight the First World War.

living standard The way in which people can afford to live.

militants People with aggressive, outspoken attitudes, especially when supporting a cause.

minister A person in charge of a department of the government.

piecework A system of producing goods where a worker is paid for each finished item.

racial discrimination Treating people unfairly because of their skin colour or race.

rationed Shared out in fixed amounts. During the Second World War, many kinds of food, petrol and clothing were rationed.

Red Cross A voluntary organization that provides emergency medical help to anyone in need.

republicans People who want their country to be ruled by a government elected by ordinary citizens and not ruled by a king or queen.

revolution A rebellion which overthrows a government.

revolutionary Someone who wants to bring about big changes in society or government, often by force.

right wing Having mostly conservative (see above) political views.

riveter Worker who joins metal plates together.

senator Member of the US Senate.

settlements Community centres offering help and advice to poor people.

status Rank; position in society.

share A certificate giving the right of ownership of a small part of a company.

stock market Place where shares are bought and sold.

strike When workers refuse to work, as a protest.

suffrage The right to vote in political elections. A suffragist believed in using only peaceful means to campaign to extend the right to vote to women.

suffragettes Nickname for women who used militant tactics to fight for the right to vote; members of the WSPU (Women's Social and Political Union).

sweatshop A crowded, unhealthy workroom.

tactics Plans and schemes used to achieve a purpose.

trade union A group of workers who have joined together to demand better pay and working conditions for their members.

unemployment Being without a job.

voluntary work Work offered freely, and done without payment.

volunteer Someone who works for no pay.

welders Workers who join two pieces of metal together by using heat and/or pressure.

welfare A person's health and well-being.

welfare benefits Money from government or charity given to people in need.

White House The official home of the President of the United States.

FURTHER READING

There to be Free; Justice at the Door; Growing up With Suffrage (education packs, The Fawcett Library, 1998); for information contact The Fawcett Library, Calcutta House, Old Castle Street, London E1 7NT (http://www.lgu.ac.uk/Phil/fawcett.htm)
The Macmillan Dictionary of Women's Biography (Macmillan, 3rd edition, 1999)
Beddoe, Deidre *Discovering Women's History* (Longman, 1998)
Roberts, Elizabeth *A Woman's Place, an oral history of working class women 1890–1940* (Blackwell, 1984)
Marlow, Joyce *The Virago Book of Women and the Great War* (Virago, 1999)
Atkinson, Diane *The Suffragettes in Pictures* (Museum of London, 1996)
Powell, Bob and Westacott, Nigel *The Women's Land Army 1939–1950* (Sutton, 1997)

INDEX

Aboriginal people 11, 44, 46
African protesters 11
airwomen 15, 37, 45
Anderson, Elizabeth Garrett 22
Anderson, Marian 42
armed forces 15, 36–37
Astor, Nancy 23
Australian campaigners 11, 44

Baker, Josephine 25
Barker, Ella 29
Barnett, Ida Wells 42
Bates, Daisy 44
Bethune, Mary McLeod 21
black women's rights 21
Bolsheviks 16, 17, 46
bombing raids 40

Cannon, Annie Jump 44
careers 7, 26–27, 46
Carney, Mabel 37
Catt, Carrie Chapman 18
Cavell, Edith 13
Chanel, 'Coco' 43
Chinese protesters 10
civil rights 7, 8, 21, 35, 42, 46
Cochran, Jacqueline 37
Coleman, Bessie 45
communists 16, 17, 46

David-Neel, Alexandra 44

Depression 32–35
Earhart, Amelia 45
election rights 22–23
equal rights 6, 21, 35, 46 (see also voting rights)
evacuees 40, 46

factory work 6–7, 15, 38
fascism 30, 46
fashions 25, 41
First World War 12–15
flappers 24, 25
Frank, Anne 43

Garbo, Greta 31
Girl Guides and Scouts 20
Goldstein, Vida 11
government work 22, 39

Haig Thomas, Margaret 42
Home Front 40–41
home life, postwar 30–31

Japanese campaigners 10, 11
Jerome, Jennie 5
Joliot-Curie, Irene 45

Kollontai, Alexandra 17
Kollwitz, Kathe 43

Land Girls 39
Lange, Dorothea 33

Lenglen, Suzanne 25

Markiewicz, Countess Constance 23
media, women in 42–43
Montessori, Maria 45

Naidu, Sarojini 10
New Deal programme 34
New Zealand campaigners 11

Odette 37

Pankhurst, Emmeline 8, 9
Paul, Alice 21
peace campaigners 13
Perkins, Frances 34
Pickford, Mary 43
pioneering women 44–45
political rights 7, 8–9, 18–21
politics 22-23, 30, 31
Popova, Liubov 27
postwar life 24–27, 41

Rankin, Jeannette 22
Ransome-Kuti, Fumilayo 11
rationed supplies 41, 47
revolution 16–17, 47
Rhondda, Lady 42
Roosevelt, Eleanor 34, 35
Russian campaigners 16

Russian Revolution 16–17

Sanger, Margaret 20
Second World War 36–41
single women 27
south-east Asian campaigners 10
sportswomen 25
stock market crash 32
strikes 6, 47
suffragettes 8–9, 47
sweatshops 5, 6, 7, 47

trades unions 6, 28–29, 47
Triangle Shirtwaist disaster 7

unemployment 32–33, 47

voting rights 7, 8–9, 18–19

wartime 12–15, 36–41
Weber, Helene 22
welfare schemes 34
welfare work 20
Wilkinson, 'Red Ellen' 29
Women's Social and Political Union 8
work for women 5, 14–15, 26–27, 36–39, 41
working conditions 6–7, 14